Tehran Diaries

Raha Nik-Andish is the pen name for a writer, translator and art historian who lives in Tehran. He has written features and essays for the *London Review of Books* and the *Markaz Review*. *Tehran Diaries* is his first book.

The *London Review of Books* is Europe's leading magazine of culture and ideas. Published twice a month, it provides a space for celebrated and lesser-known writers to explore a wide variety of subjects in exhilarating detail. Since its founding in 1979, it has also featured memoir and reportage from around the world, providing support and a platform for writers and material that wouldn't otherwise have been published. Subscribers enjoy unlimited access to its complete online archive. On lrb.co.uk you'll also find a regular blog – where Raha Nik-Andish's dispatches from Iran have been appearing since January 2026 – as well as weekly podcasts, occasional documentaries, and the latest news and events from the magazine, the London Review Bookshop and the LRB Store.

TEHRAN DIARIES

Dispatches from Iran under Siege

RAHA NIK-ANDISH

First published in Great Britain in 2026 by
Profile Books Ltd
29 Cloth Fair
London
ECIA 7JQ

www.profilebooks.com

and

London Review of Books
28 Little Russell Street
London
WCIA 2HN
www.lrb.co.uk

'Under Bombardment' (March 2026), 'Waiting for War'
(February 2026) and 'A Traitor is Still a Traitor' (January 2026)
previously published in the *London Review of Books*

'A Message from the Regime' (September 2025), 'The 12-Day
War' (June 2025) and 'Looking for a Job, Living and Dying'
(May 2025) previously published in the *Markaz Review*

1 3 5 7 9 10 8 6 4 2

Typeset in Dante by MacGuru Ltd
Printed and bound in Great Britain by
CPI Group (UK) Ltd, Croydon CRO 4YY

A CIP catalogue record for this book is available from the British Library.

Our product safety representative in the EU is BGC
Sustainability & Compliance, 7 avenue du Général Leclerc,
Paris, 75014, France https://baldwinglobalconsulting.com

ISBN 978 180649 158 2
eISBN 978 1 80649 160 5

CONTENTS

A NOTE ON THE TEXT

April 2026

In the hours following the 'elimination' of Iran's Supreme Leader Ayatollah Ali Khamenei by the US and Israel on 28 February 2026, the Iranian government turned the internet off. It was the second time this year they had plunged the nation into blackout; the first was during January's national protests against the regime which resulted, according to some estimates, in more than 30,000 deaths. At the time of writing, Iran has been under blackout for more than 1,000 hours, or 45 days. It is the longest national-scale blackout since Muammar Gaddafi cut off the internet in Libya for six months during the 2011 revolution and civil war.

For a flailing regime attempting to cling to

power, an internet shutdown perhaps seems like an effective way to retain control. It's difficult to organise a challenge to government – or otherwise meaningfully participate in political life in the digital age – without access to cellular service. But in a situation of war, it's also much more difficult to organise civilian search and rescue missions, or distribute safety information – in Ukraine and in Gaza, early tactics to sow confusion and chaos during offensives by Russian and Israeli militaries included jamming networks and cutting off service. It is a policy that results in maximum control, and maximum death. Today, in Iran, Islamic Republic officials post Telegram updates about the war that almost nobody in the nation can read.

Despite the blackout, we began working on this text with Raha Nik-Andish on 4 March. We communicated through an intermediary and friend of Raha's that he – at great personal risk – intermittently managed to keep in touch with through the shutdown and siege. At the same time, government text messages rolled in on his phone, threatening action against those seeking contact with the outside world, taking pictures or documenting evidence. Meanwhile, President Donald Trump was describing the US and Israeli aerial attacks against Iran as 'the largest, most complex, most overwhelming military offensives the world has ever seen'. This was Operation Epic Fury: banks, bridges, residential buildings, a school in Minab full of children, destroyed from above. As the war raged on, the question became not so much how we would work on this text, but whether Raha was alive or safe – whatever safety means under bombardment.

Images that emerge of Iran are often tightly controlled. From the Tasnim News Agency, the Islamic Revolutionary Guard's semi-official news source, we get one side of the story. There are the mourners in Enghelab Square, thousands in black clamouring to grieve Khamenei. There are the sustained rallies in support of the regime. Alternatively, observed from above by a pilot in an F-15 jet, the view of Iran is flattened entirely: its buildings, landmarks and people are reduced to pure data, or pure target.

Raha's work is rare and important because it gives us Iran as a multitude of worlds. Through his work, we receive a view of a society that is not a static assemblage of clichés but shifting and dynamic. It is an intensely human portrait of a place amid moments of tenderness, hope, disaster and fear. Iran is fractured and embattled but it continues to exist.

This book starts with the death of Khamenei and the beginning of Operation Epic Fury and then traces backwards. There is the war, the chaos of death, the smoke after a direct hit, but there are also the days and weeks leading up to it, the waiting, the rationing, the economic crisis and growing social division.

In going backwards, we attempt to ask how we got here. Despite signs of a tentative ceasefire negotiation in early April 2026, war is the ongoing reality in Iran, and across the Middle East – in Lebanon, Gaza and the Gulf. But before war, and during it, there was life too. This book is Raha Nik-Andish's record of that life, and an archive for the future.

INTRODUCTION
HELL HAS ARRIVED

March 2026

On Saturday 28 February at 10 a.m., my mother calls to tell me to turn on the satellite channels: the US and Israel are attacking Iran.

On Iran International TV (IITV), a Persian-language channel based in London, a woman citizen journalist reports from Tehran as smoke from a missile strike rises in the background. Her voice is filled with unmistakable joy: Ayatollah Khamenei's house has been demolished. They don't know if he's dead yet. Scrolling for more news updates, I tune in to different satellite channels as well as turning on official state TV. The state channel doesn't say anything at all; nobody else has any more updates.

At night, IITV confirms it: the Supreme Leader is dead. Yet when I turn back to the state channel, it continues its normal programming of upbeat television series as though nothing momentous is happening.

Upon hearing the news, I open my window. Everyone in the high-rise apartment buildings around me and across Tehran has come out onto their balconies. An entire nation is taken by surprise. At first, it seems inconceivable that he has been assassinated on the first day of the war. 'Maybe this is the will of God,' I hear my neighbour say from his balcony. Many Iranians believed that the Supreme Leader, despite his age, would live forever.

Completely empty streets suddenly fill with people. It's a party. People shout and honk their horns. That night, I go out to drive for Snapp!, a ride-hail service, taking people from one rushed gathering to another.

One journey takes me past a group of Basij militia, the volunteer paramilitaries. The passenger in my car smiles at them and starts laughing. Their response is quick and brutal: they smash the car's windows with their truncheons and hit the man on the back of the head.

The next morning, 1 March, I wake to the sound of the Qur'an from the loudspeakers of my local mosque, a prominent one in the city. I immediately switch on state TV. A black ribbon decorates a portrait of Ayatollah Ali Khamenei. The news of his death has finally been officially acknowledged by the regime.

I leave my building and head out into the street. Outside a man stands motionless staring at the sky. Two fighter jets move effortlessly through the clouds. He glances at me and says, with irony, 'Hell has arrived'.

Once it finished with the Qur'an, the mosque nearby began blaring songs from the Iran–Iraq war, and about the seventh-century battle of Karbala, in which the Prophet Muhammad's grandson Hussain was martyred. Overnight, new posters of Khamenei have been plastered over the city, with the words 'Martyr Leader' emblazoned beneath him. At the request of the government, religious people have begun gathering in the city squares to mourn. They cry and heave in supposed collective grief. Among everyone else, the mood is lighter. On my way to the supermarket, two shopkeepers regale passers-by: 'Go back to the front line!' They are both laughing, enjoying themselves.

I live near one of the larger squares. Every day like clockwork, from 9 p.m. to midnight, crowds of the regime's Basiji supporters gather en masse to shout anti-US and anti-Israeli slogans. This is the government's attempt to bully ordinary Iranians into silence. However, for the majority of us, their songs and slogans are meaningless. We've heard them ad infinitum since 1979.

Once the Basiji go home, precious silence once again reigns in our neighbourhood.

Ever since he was killed, paintings of Khamenei have appeared in the city. Everywhere you look, you can see this kind of stencil-style graffiti. Under them, there are short phrases: 'Superman of Iran', 'Father of the Nation'. There are even some pictures of his son, Mojtaba.

When I walk past one of the paintings again, someone has covered up Khamenei's face with garden soil.

II

After ten days of war, the sounds of the explosions and bombings have almost become normal. When will it end? And where are our leaders? State TV has no information: it broadcasts war propaganda or mourning dirges for its dead spiritual commander.

On the streets, people talk about Iran's missiles and their failure to prevent US and Israeli attacks. A friend tells me, Khamenei's death is akin to targeting the brain; the rest of the body loses control and coordination. He and I watch US fighters and drones in the skies above us. On the ground, my friend believes that one group is running the country and another is fighting the war, and neither side knows what the other is doing. Meanwhile, this fairy tale of the return of Reza Pahlavi, the son of the last Shah and the prince on a white horse, is fading fast.

At 1.46 a.m., I receive a text message from the government: Mojtaba Khamenei is the new spiritual leader of Iran.

III

Nearly two weeks into the war, one of my sisters, with her daughter and our mother, came over for dinner. As we prepared the food, two intense explosions shook the building. We didn't know where we could hide. My sister was extremely frightened and held tightly onto her daughter's hand. In a panic she kept calling to my mother in the kitchen to make sure she was OK. My mom, sitting on the floor, yelled back, 'I'm fine, I'm fine.'

The blast wave shattered two of my windows. Thick smoke rose outside as an unusually strong wind moved eastward through the streets.

Later, on Nowruz, the Persian New Year, my family joined me again. To celebrate, we prepared a *Haftseen* table with ritual foods. All of them start with the letter *sin*, a soft 's' – *senjed* (the fruit of the lotus tree or oleaster) for wisdom;

seeb (apple) for beauty; *sabzeh* (green sprouts) for rebirth and renewal; *samanu* (sweet wheat pudding) for power and strength; *seer* (garlic) for health; *serkeh* (vinegar) for age and patience and *somāq* (crushed sumac berries) for sunrise, that moment of transition from darkness to light.

But we had no such transition this year. Like every gathering these days, the festivities were punctuated by bombardment. As we stood around admiring the table, two intense explosions shook the building.

Nobody moved. Our fear was palpable. Then, my niece, who is only twelve, broke the tension. 'Don't be afraid', she told the adults and began to laugh.

Now that my windows are smashed, I have no escape from the sounds of the Basiji in the mosque. To be honest, I don't know what is worse, the sounds of the bombing or the Basijis' pleas for God's mercy. While they are blasting prayers, all I can think about is the blood of ordinary people on the streets after every aerial attack.

When I woke up the next day, someone was playing piano in a neighbour's flat. For a brief second, it seemed like a normal morning in Tehran. Then explosions from five heavy bombs are a stark reminder.

IV

The war has exacerbated another problem that Iranians have to manage: inflation. The economy was already in free fall, but now prices have doubled even compared to last month. Before, you might have been able to buy items at the supermarket. Now you have to check prices and not be surprised by a triple price increase. The challenge is trying to find the lowest-quality food, which is at the cheapest price. Still, there are plenty of fruit and vegetables in the supermarket that no one can afford. This is another kind of famine.

After the Nowruz holiday the government announced that schools and universities would be held online using the government's own internal internet. At the same time, they have outlawed practices as basic as photography. My phone constantly lights up with text messages:

> If a person attempts to take a picture of a sensitive site or building, he or she can be detained. Therefore, if you see this taking place, you are required to send the matter immediately to Ministry of Intelligence Official.

It is unclear how universities can continue teaching arts or journalism courses when documenting the war is outlawed.

People are scared and believe the country is no longer secure. The attack on the South Pars gas field, followed by Trump's repeated threats to target Iran's nuclear power plants unless the Strait of Hormuz is reopened, mark a dangerous escalation. When, after forty days of continual bombing, he threatened to send Iran back to the Stone Age, I saw fear in people's eyes. You can't imagine the effect of knowing that someone wants to kill you, and that everyone is waiting to die.

After he said that, I couldn't sleep. I got out

of bed and looked out the window. All the lights inside the flats of the surrounding buildings were on. Everyone was awake, watching the news. IITV was keeping a countdown of how long until Trump's deadline.

How much more are we expected to endure? If gas is cut off, how are people supposed to cook or keep warm? If the nuclear facilities are destroyed, we will all be thrown into darkness. Trump's repeated 48-hour ultimatums, with bridges and other infrastructure next in the line of attack, amount to collective punishment.

I have taped up my living room windows to protect them. When I check them again, I notice what a poor job I've done. I must have been nervous. Some of the tape doesn't even stick to the glass. I also notice something I hadn't seen before: my niece has stuck her cartoon stickers all along them.

I get through to my friend's phone in another country: *Tomorrow Trump plans to bomb the electricity plants.* If that happens, I will no longer be able to charge my phone and will lose all contact with the world.

1

UNDER BOMBARDMENT

March 2026

I had gone to the bank to get cash when a sudden explosion shook the building. Windows shattered and people fell to the ground. Officials shouted for everyone to leave. Outside, the streets were shrouded in thick black smoke. The bomb had landed two hundred metres away, destroying a police station, which collapsed on a bus filled with passengers. Pedestrians on the pavement were killed instantly. Among the abandoned cars, broken glass and concrete, I could see dead bodies. There must have been fifty of them. Blood was everywhere. The soldiers at the scene ordered me to leave.

Most of the time we don't see the civilians killed by the US and Israeli bombs. From our rooftops we watch plumes of smoke rise over buildings. The internet is down. There are no journalists. When the bomb hit the police station near the bank, I just happened to be close by.

The sounds of planes and drones are always in my ears. When I hear the roar of a motorcycle I think it's a drone. Even the noise of the lift moving between the floors of my building makes me think the city is being bombed.

No one knows how long this war will go on. No matter how many regime commanders the US and Israel kill from the air, they will only be replaced and the regime will carry on. My friend Jamal says the war is like Russia's war on Ukraine. Another friend, Babek, compares Israel and America to beauticians who remove eyebrow hair. They pluck carefully, hair by hair, until the moment they decide to shave the whole eyebrow off.

Some people I know support the war and some are vehemently against it. A bipolar friction runs through friends and families – caught between outrage and exhaustion. The opponents talk about the killing of civilians, the loss of cultural heritage, the degradation of the environment. The supporters believe there is no other way to change the regime and free the people. Some of those who wanted the Americans and the Israelis to bomb Iran have changed their minds since the war started. Iranians in the diaspora want war but those of us living it first-hand are frightened.

The only credible Persian news comes from the satellite channels based in London. When the government jams the frequency, I pay for the receiver to be retuned. State television says only that the regime is winning.

No one goes out to protest anymore. It's far too dangerous. I was talking to another friend, a schoolmate during the war with Iraq, remembering how during air raids we would hide in our school's underground shelter. It's completely different now: everyone lives in high-rise apartment blocks and there are no warning sirens.

My cousin's house and car were badly damaged in the blast wave from a bombing. He asked for support from the government. The authorities offered him a loan but he would never be able to pay it back. One of my sisters has moved her family to the countryside outside Tehran.

After the bombing of the police station I realised there's no way of knowing how much danger you may be in. People say the Revolutionary Guards are afraid to stay in their own buildings and have started hiding in schools. It's better to stay at home. We might not know who's hiding where but maybe the Israelis and the Americans do.

My mother called and said: 'Look outside, look at the sky.' An hour earlier we had heard four or five explosions. I looked outside. Thickening smoke obscured the night sky and the air smelled of oil.

2

WAITING FOR WAR

February 2026

Usually, the last days of February are filled with anticipation of the Persian New Year holiday, Nowruz. People shop for new clothes, grocery stalls brim with mounds of oranges, mothers bargain for tiny goldfish in water-filled plastic bags. Tehran used to move faster at this time of year. People spoke with more confidence, even the smog seemed less suffocating. But this year, the city is on pause.

My friend, who recently defended her doctoral dissertation, invited a few of us to her home. When she opened the door, I said, 'Tehran seems silent. Where is everyone?'

She gestured at the street vendor selling wares outside on the pavement. 'See that woman? Every night she calls the municipality, asking them whether the Americans will attack tonight.' She paused, her voice softer now. 'Nobody is planning for the New Year; they are planning for the day after an attack.'

At the gathering, no one spoke about a future career. Conversations orbited an invisible centre. One person mapped an escape route. Another discussed hoarding cash. A third mentioned the need to fill her car with petrol before dark. A few days ago, withdrawing cash from an ATM was effortless; now machines are often empty, or dispense limited sums. Nothing has been formally announced but a shift has taken place. People move their savings out of banks and change rials into dollars. Transactions take place discreetly, and banks release cash cautiously. Scarcity is a lesson in restraint.

My sister calls me every day. She's worried about the costly meat in her freezer going bad if the electricity is turned off. She then asks the same question, 'Have you stocked up yet?'

She has stored enough food and water for two weeks.

At her insistence, I go to the supermarket. Bottled water has vanished from the pavement outside the store. The store's owner told me, 'We don't have quotas – just one or two bottles per person.' On the shelves, candles and batteries were scarce.

On social media, we are told to buy tinned fish and beans, any food that will last. But prices have risen so much. In the end I can only afford two tins of tuna – not enough to cover my needs. By the front door, next to my slippers and outside shoes, I stuff a bag full of all my important documents. I check my things: do I have enough water, cash, candles and petrol to drive for Snapp! In the morning before people go to work, they test batteries and flashlights instead of checking emails.

These days, my mother is more silent than usual. For the news she keeps official state TV on in the background but watches Instagram on her phone. The reels posted by the Iranian satellite channels in London – Iranian

International TV, Manoto and BBC Persian – show the fortieth-day commemorations for the victims killed during the January protests.

Instead of the traditional black, many mourners wear white. Almost all of them clap and dance by their loved ones' graves. The Islamic prayers and elegies have been replaced by traditional drumming music from southern Iran, or songs by local singers or singers popular before the revolution. One reel shows a nearly collapsed, middle-aged man – perhaps a father – stricken by grief, barely held up by his relations, yet his arms wave feebly in time to the music. It made my mother cry. Dancing has always been a mainstay of Persian family get-togethers; now dancing in grave-yards has become a sign of defiance.

At my university, where I teach part-time, undergraduate classes are again online. Graduate classes are still in person, which may account for the number of students protesting on Tehran campuses. Protestors have renamed Sharif University of Technology 'Prince Arya-mehr', after Shah Mohammad Reza Pahlavi. A stuffed toy mouse dangles from the branch of a tree to represent a scared Supreme Leader Ayatollah Khamenei, at that time still in hiding. During the demonstration, students were attacked by members of the pro-regime Basij militia. Later, one clambered up the tree and freed the stuffed toy mouse and protestors mocked him: 'Cry, Basiji, cry!'

After the crackdown on the Green Movement demonstrations in 2009, it took two years before people dared to go out on the streets again. This time it has been only weeks.

Rumours abound. In the hallway of my college, a colleague stopped me and said that some students committed suicide after the protests. Others are admittedly nervous. 'Before we were worried about grades,' one told me, 'now we're worried about surviving two weeks without electricity or water.' Even children understand the gravity of the situation. My eleven-year-old niece calls me to say, 'Uncle, let's agree to meet in a place, in case the phones don't work.'

During the month of Ramadan, after the

evening call to prayer, people usually fill the res-taurants or cafés. Now, out driving for Snapp!, I've noticed how empty the grocery stores are. One evening, a passenger with two children got in. After a long silence, he said, 'We protested for our kids' future, now everyone negotiates only for themselves and their own interests.'

'Are you afraid of war?' I asked.

'No,' he replied. 'I fear that life will continue the same afterwards.'

At midnight, I picked up a young woman, a university lecturer. 'Students have no hope,' she told me. 'War or no war won't alter their feelings.'

I dropped her off and then parked by a flower stall. Next to the blooms, a street singer held a microphone. Her voice was strong and resonant, as she sang an old song by Hayedeh that is officially banned. 'Year after year, regret is all we have.'

None of the people who gathered to watch her applauded. No one filmed. They simply listened.

3

A TRAITOR IS STILL A TRAITOR

January 2026

For eighteen days now, I have been cut off from the virtual world – not by choice, not as a form of digital detox, but by force. I've been living in a kind of solitary confinement whose walls are invisible but whose population numbers 90 million people. It is a prison where no sound goes out and no image gets through. Every attempt to send a message, a video, or even a simple sentence has failed.

My voice was cut off on 8 January, after I sent a video of the rice protests to a friend in England. Suddenly, everything went dark.

That day, Reza Pahlavi had issued a message calling on people to come out into the streets at eight in the evening, in response to the catastrophic economic situation and the strikes that had begun in the bazaars a week earlier.

I live on the top floor of an apartment building in western Tehran. I turned off the lights and through my windows watched the city below. It was slowly changing shape. Shops were closing one by one. The streets had taken on a suspended quality, as if the city was holding its breath.

In the darkness, I saw young people running like shadows, stopping, turning back and running again. Each time, their numbers grew, like streams merging until they formed a wide, powerful river. My phone rang. It was a friend. He said, 'We're going to Qeytarieh Square. Come with us.'

We headed northeast by car. Along the way, shopkeepers were hurriedly pulling down their shutters, like scenes from an old Hollywood western. The city was preparing itself for confrontation.

When we arrived, I couldn't believe the crowds. These neighbourhoods have always been thought to be wealthy – people never usually protested. But economic pressure had erased the distinction between upper and lower classes. Discontent had become universal.

The chants were loud: 'Long live the Shah,' 'Death to Khamenei.' A few of us tried to stay together and move as a group, but it quickly became clear that my friends preferred to remain in the safer parts of the crowd. I wanted to know what was happening further ahead – why waves of fear kept pushing people back.

I moved forward. People had piled sandbags and dirt in the middle of the street. Road signs and alley nameplates had been torn down to block the entry of security forces. Someone poured petrol onto a pile of tires, and flames rose high, lighting up the street.

Across from us stood riot police in full gear, twenty or thirty of them, along with armed plainclothes agents. I looked at the protesters around me. Most of them were very young, perhaps twenty years old: girls and boys dressed in dark clothes, faces covered with masks to hide their identities, ready to escape into the darkness. People warned one another: 'Don't go into side alleys. You'll get trapped.'

Tear gas was fired. The chants continued. Someone shouted, 'They're shooting!' We all ran. A young woman stopped and asked me to look at the back of her neck. She had been hit by pellets.

The sound of gunfire intensified. I could see flashes in the darkness and didn't understand what they were. (Later, when the internet came back on and videos surfaced on Instagram, I realised that the authorities had been firing directly into the crowd.)

Seeing the young woman who had already been shot was enough for me. I headed back towards my friend's car. To avoid identification none of us had brought our phones, so there was no way for us to be in touch. But my friends were waiting for me.

We drove back to west Tehran, towards Sadeghieh Square. The streets were filled with fire. We tried to take different routes, where there were fewer demonstrations. Near the square, the crowds grew large. I got out of the car and ran towards home.

Suddenly, I found myself in the middle of a violent clash. Plainclothes agents were attacking people with batons. The sound of gunfire did not stop. Wounded protesters were being carried away by others.

By the side of the road, a plainclothes agent was sitting on top of the body of a very young boy. The agent's arm seemed to be moving up and down, yet he held no baton. I moved a little closer. He was stabbing the boy with a knife. I turned around and ran.

It took me half an hour to reach home. I was worried about my family, but the phone and internet weren't working. In the flat, I didn't dare turn on a light. From the window, I watched the gunfire and tear gas below. Around three in the morning, the city finally fell silent.

People were supposed to return to the streets again at eight the following evening. At dusk, around five o'clock, the shops began closing. The security forces were out in far greater numbers.

I didn't feel well. The thought of leaving home without my phone again felt impossible. I watched from my window. I could see riot motorcycles and armoured vehicles with three men in the back, one of them standing behind a mounted machine gun. A few hours later the sound of gunfire was so intense that it felt like a war zone. There was shouting and chants – and screaming.

On 10 January, I went to buy bread. Bakeries are usually places of quiet conversation, but on that day anger was visible on people's faces. The queue was long, and in the span of one hour I witnessed two serious altercations.

ATMs were not working. The internet was still down. Ride-hailing services had stopped. You could make phone calls but not send texts. The only incoming messages were from the government:

Following public demands for firm action against those disrupting security, citizens

are requested to report any suspicious indi-
viduals or elements threatening security by
calling 114, 113 or 110.

This was followed by:

Dear parents, due to the enemy's plan to
increase open violence and deliberately
cause civilian deaths, please remain alert
to these plots and avoid being present in
streets or gatherings where violence is
taking place. Also, inform your children
about the consequences of cooperating
with terrorist mercenaries, which is consid-
ered an act of betrayal against the country.
 – IRGC Intelligence Organisation

And then:

Report any suspicious activity.

The same people who had been called
'rioters' the day before were now labelled 'ter-
rorists'. Additional warnings were issued: any

contact with the outside world or sharing of images would be met with severe punishment.

A few days later, my brother called me. 'There's no good news,' he said. 'I heard that our cousin has been arrested.'

I live near one of the Islamic Revolutionary Courts, which handle alleged threats to national security. The day after the protests began, two to three hundred people gathered outside the courthouse daily.

A man reported that his son, a soldier, had been arrested on his way to the barracks. Judges were issuing verdicts based on interrogation reports. Did he have videos? Did he throw stones? Punishment could be a fine, starting at 80 million tomans, followed by property confiscation, prison sentences, or even death.

We still have no news of my cousin. We only know that he has been detained.

On 13 January, Iran International satellite television announced – based on its investigations – that over the course of just two days, twelve thousand people had been killed. They broadcast horrifying images from the Kahrizak

Medical Forensic Centre, showing bodies piled on top of one another. BBC Persian, more cautiously, spoke of thousands of deaths. Iranian state television initially announced a figure of two thousand. Two weeks later, some unofficial estimates placed the number killed at more than 36,500.

In the absence of reliable information, rumours became a parallel reality. Numbers circulated quietly, whispered in queues and inside cars, repeated without certainty but with conviction. What everyone knew for sure was that death had entered daily life.

I had stopped driving for Snapp! on 8 January. It just didn't seem safe and I was scared to go back to driving nights. But a few days later I hailed one to go to the cinema, to try to change my state of mind. Because it was a long ride, I asked the driver to turn on the radio. He scoffed and said, 'I've boycotted radio and television. They assume we're idiots and lie to us.'

His main job, he told me, was driving an ambulance, but since one job was no longer enough to survive, he had started working for Snapp! On 10 January, he had been on duty. 'Just me alone,' he said, 'I transported four hundred bodies to Kahrizak.'

He spoke calmly, almost mechanically, as though by repeating the story it was no longer deeply upsetting. 'The scenes I saw will stay with me for the rest of my life. Over those two days – 8 and 9 of January – they killed so many people that bodies were stored in mosques.'

Then he added, without raising his voice, 'I can say this comfortably: they killed 100,000 people.'

He told me about a woman who came to collect her husband's body. According to those accompanying her, the man had leaned out of a window to look at what was happening when he was shot in the head. His body fell into the street. From above, his wife and daughter watched as security forces placed his body into a black bag and carried it away. The wife ran downstairs. When she touched her husband's blood on the pavement, it was still warm. Her daughter had stopped speaking.

When the woman went to the morgue, the authorities demanded payment for the bullet. She showed them a cloth soaked in her husband's blood and said she would bury the bloodied cloth herself – and that they could keep the body.

Tehran is in mourning. You do not hear music or laughter. Every person who was killed had a family, and all families are connected. In a way, all of Iran has suffered a death. The grief is collective, heavy and unspoken.

In this collapsed economy, perhaps the only people who continue to earn an income are sellers of dates, halva and candles – because at mourning ceremonies it is customary to distribute dates and halva, and to burn candles, constantly, in homes and on pavements.

At the cinema, I watched an Iranian comedy. *Aghaye Zalo* is about a former dealer in alcohol who falls in love with a woman from a prominent government family. It was funny on the surface, but the audience's laughter was tinged with irony and sadness. After forty-seven years of the Islamic Republic, these everyday absurdities have become grotesque enough to be repackaged simply as entertainment.

I had arranged to meet friends in a café and took a shared taxi to get there. The woman alongside me was religious and kept muttering blessings – *salavat* – under her breath. She announced that she was praying for conditions to improve.

'Our problem as people is that we throw everything into God's court,' the driver said. 'God gave us the tools for life. The rest must be managed with reason. Nothing gets fixed with prayers and blessings.'

When I got out, his words stayed with me. For forty-seven years, the words 'Death to America, England and Israel' have been shouted at Friday prayers, using God and religion to mobilise people, while pushing society and the economy to a point where humanity itself has eroded, and where fear of hunger makes everyone think only of how to empty the pockets of others.

At the café, the mood among my friends was not good. I asked one how business was. He owns a women's clothing store in the bazaar. 'I closed the shop,' he said. 'There are no sales at all. Like you, I've started driving Snapp! at six in the morning and work until ten at night. Maybe I get two hours of rest in between. I make about 20 million rials a day, 600 million a month. My rent is 280 million rials. Food prices go up every day. How am I supposed to live?'

He said people think America is coming with warships to overthrow the clerics. 'They're not coming for that. They're coming to stop oil exports. Even if we sell oil, they don't pay cash. They give us Chinese goods. What use are cars to us? We need money, not barter.'

'If America attacks Iran,' I said, 'won't people be killed?'

'They don't kill people. Our own government does. No enemy in our history has done to us what these clerics have done.'

But not everybody agreed. My friend Koshrow said: 'People have forgotten history. The same people who are now waiting for an American attack have forgotten that during the Iran–Iraq war, people were praying for an end.

They used to say that even if we went hungry, it would be better than continuing the war.'

I said: 'But the regime behaves like the Taliban. Do you want to stay in prison?'

Koshrow paused and stirred his tea. 'No one loves a prison,' he said. 'But if a snake bites you once, you don't put your hand back into the same hole. War doesn't tear down the prison walls, it only makes the roof collapse on the prisoners.'

'It's not going to be an equal fight where we take ten hits and give ten back,' said another friend. 'We always take ten hits and give one or two.' He said that the Iranian navy had been training for years in the water; they would welcome a confrontation at sea.

Everyone discussed this in a way that made it seem inevitable. It was a crisp day. Spring was in the air. We were sitting by the café door and blowing smoke out onto the street. Elsewhere in the city, a new billboard towers over a busy highway. On one side is a black-and-white photo of Abolhassan Banisadr, the first president after the revolution, who was impeached in 1981. On the other is a colour photo of Masih Alinejad, a journalist who left Iran in 2009 and is now a US citizen and prominent critic of the regime. Between them are the words: 'A traitor is still a traitor.'

4

DRIVING IN THE DARK

January 2026

Six months ago, I thought about buying a car, not for convenience but out of necessity. My rate of pay as a freelance university lecturer is 30,000 tomans (300,000 IRR) per hour, roughly $0.22 USD. The sum barely covers my daily commute. I thought I could drive at night for the ride-hailing service Snapp! to at least cover my basic living expenses. I had enough savings to buy a hatchback Saipa Quik – but then its price went up 66 per cent.

I wasn't able to buy a car, but I still drive for Snapp! One-third of my earnings goes to the car's owner, Snapp! takes a commission, and I pay for the car's wear and tear as well as fuel. Being a driver is a temporary survival strategy rather than a sustainable way of life. When I pick up fares at night, I worry that one of my students will get into the back of the car and ask why their lecturer is driving for Snapp!

Night-time driving means I have short conversations with passengers that are frank and unfiltered. During these past months, I hardly met anyone who is content with the economy or at peace with the future. Fear and anxiety have become constants.

One night I picked up a pair of estate agents. One suddenly asked, 'Is working with Snapp! profitable? Everyone seems to be doing it.'

I smiled bitterly and said that I was just starting.

He replied: 'What this government has done to Iran's economy no enemy could have accomplished. They frighten the people. So money goes into gold and coins. Then inflation rises and the gold is dumped back into the market. It's a dirty economic game to empty people's pockets.'

When I asked about the housing market, he said, 'It's not about having money. It's about instability. Nobody dares to sell or buy. Prices can shift so fast that you might not even be able to buy back your own home.' Later, I heard similar sentiments from shopkeepers, office workers, even government employees.

I work for Snapp! three times a week, from around 11 p.m. to 3 a.m., mostly so I can pay for food. One night as I was walking home from my local supermarket, I passed two men standing beside a car. One pointed at my plastic carrier bag. 'How much did that cost?' he asked. 'You must be rich!'

'You don't even know what's inside,' I told him. I had only bought essentials: yoghurt, cheese, rice, lentils, soap and shampoo.

'It looks like one-third of my pension,' he said.

A few steps along, a woman seated on a bench asked me, 'Sir, will you give me your yoghurt?'

These days, begging for food is not unusual. Frequently, those asking are elderly people, forced to survive on relatively little.

At the university, fewer students have been on campus because of repeated closures by the government. Last week universities were closed from Thursday to Sunday to prevent illegal gatherings or protests. There are only two weeks left until the end of term. For students not taking exams, classes will be taught online. Some of the students I teach have said they will boycott their exams in solidarity with the protests. Nationwide, slogans such as 'The student dies, he does not accept humiliation', 'No Gaza, no Lebanon, my life for Iran', and even anti-government shouts like 'Death to Khamenei' and 'Javid Shah' (Long Live the Shah) have surfaced on campus.

On 28 December, shopkeepers in Tehran's Grand Bazaar shut their stores in protest at financial hardship, with videos circulating online showing quiet streets and shuttered storefronts – a powerful symbol of economic revolt. The protests, strikes and sit-ins in Tehran quickly spread to Shiraz, Isfahan, Mashhad, Hamadan and other cities. Those involved were market traders, students and ordinary citizens. Some demonstrations in Isfahan and Mashhad have explicitly linked demands for basic welfare with broader calls for freedom and systemic change.

The demonstrations are in some ways a continuation of the Woman, Life, Freedom protests from 2022, except that now they go beyond the issue of gender and the hijab. Today, many women forego headscarves anyway.

The security forces have attempted to break up demonstrations – sometimes using tear gas or worse, live ammunition – yet many people have stood their ground. In some of the pro-tests, people engaged with police officers in the streets, discussing their economic hardships and trying to persuade the police to stand with rather than against them. Twenty-one people were killed this month, with over one thou-sand injured and two thousand arrested. Still, compared to the levels of violence during the Woman, Life, Freedom demonstrations, the government is seemingly searching for a way out. They promised to distribute food vouch-ers to every Iranian citizen to help with buying staples, but people remain sceptical. Masked demonstrators in the city of Abdanan attacked a Revolutionary Guards discount chain store and threw rice on the streets to protest at high food prices and government corruption. The regime also announced a change in the official exchange rate with the dollar, to align it more closely with the black market rate that everyone uses. According to a government spokesman, this means that the price of food – including cooking oil, which has become increasingly scarce – will rise even further.

Meanwhile, a widely shared documentary about the Iranian actress Taraneh Alidoosti by BBC Persian (which is banned in Iran) has garnered significant attention on YouTube. In it, Alidoosti recounts her arrest during the Woman, Life, Freedom protests and a rare skin shedding condition she developed after her release from Evin Prison. These stories from the women's prisons are not uncommon. I know someone whose hair has fallen out and not grown back. In the interview, Alidoosti declares that she will no longer appear in films in a headscarf – both a rejection of the country's compulsory dress codes and a sign of her belief in individual freedom.

There has been a widespread reaction to the documentary on social media, with many people saying that Alidoosti was expressing not just personal but collective pain, speaking to the frustrations of many Iranians struggling under economic and social hardship.

During the protests, whether in an attempt to win local hearts and minds or to lay the groundwork for international retribution against the regime, online imagery has played a crucial role. One image shows a man sitting in an Iranian street facing security forces, in an echo of the famous 'tank man' from the Chinese protests of Tiananmen Square. But it's difficult to know what is real, and what has been created by AI. The BBC showed that a widely circulated photograph of two protesters in Hamadan being sprayed by a riot policeman with a water cannon had been AI-generated. It was posted on the Persian-language X account of the Israeli government.

What is real are the helicopters hovering in the skies over my head and their constant surveillance. I have trouble sleeping at night; I live in a suspended state of tension. When I told my mother to stock up on staples, she looked at me serenely. Her generation has lived through revolution and war. She has seen worse.

For a while now I've had the feeling that we're on the *Titanic*, and I'm not the only one. A video on Instagram, shared by 120,000 people, shows a black-and-white montage of ordinary Iranian streets as a mournful Leonard Cohen sings: 'Everybody knows the boat is leaking, everybody knows the captain lied …' When I'm driving for Snapp! I go past people searching through the garbage for metal to sell.

The other night, I picked up my last passenger from the airport at around three in the morning. He carried a small suitcase, and was on his way home. He looked like he was about seventy years old. His voice was calm, but his face carried the weight of many years. I wanted to talk to him: I mentioned the exchange rate, which is the highest it's ever been.

He looked at me in the rear-view mirror and said, 'I have a request. I will speak, and you don't answer. Even if you think I'm wrong, just listen.'

He paused, before continuing, 'This is the result of what people did in 1979 when they shouted "Death to the Shah" and handed the country to people who knew nothing about politics or the world. They were supposed to pray, not run a nation. When you give the fate of a country to superstition and ignorance, this is what you get.'

He fell silent as the traffic light turned red. Then, he added more quietly, 'But remember: no government lasts forever. Everything has its time. Their time will end too. The world, with all its detours, eventually moves forward.'

Then I dropped him at his house, and he melted away. I turned off the motor and sat quietly by myself for a few moments, the exchange rate of the dollar rising and falling in my head. My phone lit up on the dashboard; it was the request for a new ride.

I didn't answer it. Not yet. My hand rested on the steering wheel as I looked down the empty unlit street. It felt as if I had been driving in the dark for years. Then I started the engine and drove off. We're still moving not because we know where we're going, but because stopping is no longer an option.

5

A MESSAGE FROM THE REGIME

September 2025

There were several new developments in Iran's cultural and urban landscape following the end of the 12-Day War. On the surface, they at first seemed scattered, but taken together they appeared to be part of a broader strategy aimed at boosting public morale and repairing the government's image. From the renewed prominence of nationalist symbols in public spaces to the display of artworks once banned or marginalised in museums – even inviting expatriate cultural practitioners back home – these moves signalled fresh efforts on the part of the regime to revive hope in a society still reeling from the war with Israel.

In Tehran's Vanak Square, in the north of the city, they have installed a new sculpture of Arash the Archer. In Persian mythology, Arash (whose name means 'bright' or 'luminescent' in Farsi) fired an arrow, and where it fell defined the country's borders. The 15-metre bronze statue, by Mohammad Dehghan Mohammadi, the son of renowned Iranian sculptor Iraj Mohammadi, also has a new imposing backdrop nearby. An unmissable mural, covering most of a building that looms over a bus station and taxi rank, shows missiles launched alongside Arash's timeless arrow. This pointedly curated public space suggests that both military prowess and ancient myth now share the duty of guarding Iranian borders.

There is a YouTube video interview between the pre-revolution pop star Shahram Shabpareh, based in the US, and the popular talk show host Ali Zia that has gone viral online. In the interview, Shabpareh talks about the hardships of life in America, such as high insurance costs and social insecurity. Some critics said that Shabpareh was ignoring the realities of migration, and others also took issue with the fact that he was permitting himself to be interviewed by Zia, a presenter formerly affiliated with state media. In a later media appearance, Shabpareh reiterated his disdain for the government that had forced him into exile.

Lately, the newly elected president Masoud Pezeshkian has spoken of creating the conditions for the return of Iranians abroad. Despite the arrest of returnees in the past, Pezeshkian urged the judiciary and the intelligence services to coordinate in order to allow those who were homesick back into the country after some forty-seven years in exile.

These signals from the government, combined with their sponsorship of public art and culture, are part of concerted attempts to offer both a semblance of historical continuity and psychological stability to a domestic public that has not only been wounded by the war but shaken by the arrests of some of their neighbours mistakenly identified by the regime as collaborators with Israel.

One of the most high-profile cultural efforts of recent weeks has been the exhibition 'In Women's Words', at the Tehran Museum of Contemporary Art (TMOCA), which opened in July and features works by pioneering Iranian women artists from the years preceding the 1979 Iranian Revolution. According to the exhibition literature, 'The diversity of works by modern Iranian women in the two decades of the 1960s and 1970s recalls an era of freedom, experimentation, and boldness, marked by pluralism and the dominance of modernism.'

On view is artwork by Behjat Sadr (1924–2009), Parvaneh Etemadi (1948–2025), Mansoureh Hosseini (1926–2012) and Farah Ossouli (b. 1953), all prominent Iranian women artists whose work younger Iranians have rarely had the chance to see. Many visitors to the TMOCA expressed delight at encountering these pioneering artists for the first time, pre-viously suppressed for their political or critical stance.

On opening day, I went with a friend who wasn't wearing a headscarf. I told her they might not let her in. She shrugged: 'If there's a problem, I'll just throw my shirt over my head.'

At the museum entrance, as predicted, two female security guards in chadors told women whose hair was visible that they needed to wear a covering. Most complied with a scarf or a piece of clothing, only to remove it once they were inside. This small but telling scene encapsulated the daily duel between officialdom and public behaviour and served to underscore a bifurcated social psyche. Iranians live split lives, where what is said and done in private cannot always be repeated outside, on pain of punishment – or sometimes even death.

The exhibition featured video pieces by the exiled artist Shirin Neshat, who left Iran in 1974 to study art in California and returned briefly to visit the country in 1990. In her work *Turbulent* (1998), traditional male singer Shoja Azari sings a Persian love song to a packed auditorium on one side of a split screen. On the other, the experimental singer and composer

Sussan Deyhim, wearing a scarf, improvises, her voice echoing around the empty seats of another auditorium. In *Tooba* (2002), a woman disappears into a tree as men approach. In her art, Neshat has been known for her sharp rebukes of Iranian gender politics and power structures. Also included in the exhibition were a series of photographs by Yalda Moaiery, arrested in 2022 for covering the protests about the death of Mahsa Amini. She spent several months in prison and was then forced to clean the streets.

In another room was a piece by Zohreh Kazemi, better known as Zahra Rahnavard. Rahnavard had spent years under house arrest with her husband Mir Hossein Mousavi, who had once been the prime minister of Iran and was a famous opposition figure who had stood in the contested 2009 elections. Although she recently gave Netanyahu a public dressing-down for Israel's targeting of women and girls during the onslaught on Gaza, she has also been a long-standing and formidable critic of Iranian state policies. Her inclusion in the exhibition is a notable symbol of either a change in tone or, at the very least, a rethinking by official institutions on how to reconfigure the cultural space.

According to museum organisers, all these works had been part of the TMOCA's collection for years. At the opening, some artists admitted to me that they were unaware of when the museum had purchased their work – or whether they had ever received payment for it. One of the curators reportedly told a participating artist that 'we have no intention of excluding anyone', but when asked about restrictions imposed from outside the curatorial team, in other words the government, the curator had no answer.

Some artists told me that they had been contacted only a week before the exhibition's opening and been asked to send in a work if one were available. Another artist, with work in the museum's permanent collection, said that it was only after she had received an invitation for the opening that she realised she had been included. Given that exhibitions of this scale usually require months of planning, the hurried nature of the event was notable.

Historically, large-scale imagery in public space has been one of the mainstays of government communication with the Iranian people. During the Iran–Iraq War (1980–88), artists like Khosrow Hassanzadeh (1963–2023) painted the faces of those killed, and these became both symbols and celebrations of the ultimate sacrifice made for the country by these men and boys, their plaintive expressions staring down from buildings throughout the capital. For many, that war represents a time when, only a year after Ayatollah Khomeini had come to power, the country was on a united footing: under attack, it had been able to mobilise thousands of volunteer citizens to protect the nascent Islamic regime. While martyr murals from that period have not entirely disappeared from the urban landscape, new iterations have suddenly appeared. Cut-outs of group shots of fighters from the 1980s have been affixed to the sides of bridges. Some stare pensively at passers-by. Others appear almost jolly.

History matters to the government. Like the billboard of Arash the Archer in Vanak Square, other public art displays emphasise the connection between the politics of today and Persia's distant past. In one billboard that went viral in July, instead of the Roman emperor Valerian on his knees in humiliation and defeat before a Sasanian king, Netanyahu appears in bowed supplication to King of Kings Shapur I (r. 240–270) in a mock rock relief modelled on the one from Naqsh-e-Rostam near Persepolis, the ancient capital of the Achaemenid Empire. Another foregrounds military commanders and nuclear scientists killed in the 12-Day War against a backdrop of monarchs from different Persian dynasties, including Cyrus the Great (600–530 BC). All appear under the slogan 'We are the guardians of Iran in every era', and link contemporary figures with historical defenders of the land. New political billboards appear almost daily – they go up and down, a fluid, fluctuating visual landscape. In themselves, they represent a sudden shift in the Islamic Republic's traditional use of its nation-building narrative. For decades, the government distanced itself from the monarchy, emphasising its break with past dynasties, particularly that of Mohammad Reza Shah and his 2,500-year celebration of the monarchy as a continuous legacy. But following the 12-Day War, in the face of sudden instability, the government is now relying on Iran's royal history to connect the present-day military and scientific heroes with the glories of the past. The result is a surprising and unusual pairing of two historically opposed narratives. But they are a sedative, not a path towards lasting renewal. The state has built the billboards, but the billboards have not rebuilt the state. We remain in a place of uncertainty, exhaustion and psychological fracture.

Over a highway in Tehran, there is another banner. Emblazoned over the poster are the words: 'If Damascus falls, Tehran could be next.' It seems to be an attempted answer to a whispered question: when the economy and people are suffering so much, why is the government so involved in another regional war?

6

THE 12-DAY WAR

June 2025

It's the morning after Iran and Israel have announced a ceasefire.

As always, the anti-aircraft sirens sound tired and worn out, cutting through the night unexpectedly and pulling me, without thinking, out onto the balcony. My eyes follow the glowing trails across the sky. I spot a small bright dot far away. A drone, or something trying to escape? There is a soldier firing at it.

I look more closely: no, it's not a drone. It's a star. Still, quiet, unmoved.

These past twelve days have changed everything. We're not the same people we were before. It's like someone whose house has collapsed in an earthquake now searching through the rubble for an old diary.

And we still don't know when exactly it all began, or ended. And now we'll carry it with us for the rest of our lives, always asking: Who are we? Why did we lose? Why does the government claim victory, after so many failures?

How can someone look in a mirror, maimed and bloody, and continue to ask, 'Did you see how well I hit them?'

On the first morning of the ceasefire, the newspaper headlines had changed. Just yesterday, one paper had boldly printed a photo of a missile with the words: 'A decisive response is on the way.' Now it showed the image of an unveiled woman with the headline: 'After the storm.'

BBC Persian reported that Evin Prison had been hit by an Israeli strike. The main entrance, the women's ward, the visitation hall, the library – everything was damaged. One thousand and two hundred male prisoners were transferred to the Greater Tehran Prison. They didn't even have time to grab their clothes or bring their medication. Seven hundred female prisoners were sent without basic supplies to the vastly inferior and more dangerous Qarchak prison in the unbearable heat. So much for the Israelis' 'symbolic' bombing that was supposed to free Iran's political prisoners.

Sources close to the Revolutionary Guard said that at least 700 people were arrested during these twelve days for allegedly collaborating with Israel. Six were executed. Three of them, all Kurds, were hung in the north-western city of Urmia near the Turkish border. They were *kolbars*, porters, who carried banned goods on their back across the mountains into Iran. The Norway-based Iran Human Rights Group said that they had been initially charged with smuggling alcohol over the border but were later forced to confess to espionage.

To cover up for the massive failure of the war, the government has already begun an internal crackdown. The Revolutionary Guards and Basij – volunteer paramilitaries – were deployed to the borders, and official warnings were given of 'the danger from within', notably from the Kurdish areas of the country. The Iranian human rights agency HRNA reported that many of the people who had recently been arrested had been accused of spying for Israel. This doesn't bode well for activists already in detention.

Someone had written online: 'This war worked like a vacuum cleaner. It sucked up the dust – and the people.'

I was sitting in a dimly lit café near Valiasr Square. Someone nearby said, 'We lost. That's it.'

Another replied, 'No, militarily we won. If you compare the size of Israel and Iran, then for every missile Iran fired, Israel would've had to launch fifty to have the same impact. Iran has been under sanctions for years, and Israel wasn't alone – it had US and European support.'

A third person smirked: 'Brother, look around this city. There's no space here you could call a victory.'

More than thirty senior Iranian com-manders were killed in the war. In Israel, not a single soldier died, let alone a senior officer. It is simply the dream of victory that people believe in. My friend's father insisted that Israel had been defeated, just because it eventually stopped the attacks. He had been watching Islamic Republic of Iran Broadcasting and mimicked the TV anchorman's sense of achievement. When I told him the statistics, and how not one Israeli commander had been killed, he just smiled and said, 'What matters is willpower.' His generation had been raised on the memory of the Iran–Iraq war – on images of young boys confronting tanks. For them, 'not losing' equals 'winning'.

But people my age no longer believe in such narratives. The generational divide is real. One side still believes in patience and faith. The other side just wants a way out.

I took a long walk. The air felt heavy, as if the city itself couldn't breathe. I wandered aimlessly until I ended up in front of a computer shop known for selling Apple products, where people had lined up.

It was strange. Phones in hand, they were

waiting, not for the latest iPad or app, not for repairs, but for something that's become as essential as daily bread in Iran these days: a VPN.

I followed everyone inside.

The tired but friendly shop assistant repeated this same sentence dozens of times: 'I'll install the VPN for you, but don't think the internet's back. It's just a workaround. Maybe Instagram and WhatsApp will open – if they don't, the government has shut them down again.'

My eyes alighted on one of the store's employ-ees. He was sitting behind a monitor, repairing a small electronic motherboard. A magnified view of it was displayed on the monitor above him – complex circuit boards, the grey tones of capacitors, and hints of greenish-blue edges. I joked, 'Looking at that screen, you'd think we were in a nuclear power plant!'

The seller replied, 'Yeah, that one's heavy water. This one's probably Natanz!' (one of the nuclear facilities where the US dropped buster bombs). Despite ourselves we both laughed.

The person behind me had overheard us. He

murmured, 'Man, look what these twelve days of war have done to us … Now, whatever we see, we call it a reactor. Everything's become nuclear, become a threat.' He added pointedly, 'Where is the Supreme Leader?'

On the eighth day of the 12-Day War, on 20 June, Foreign Minister Abbas Araghchi arrived in Geneva for diplomatic talks. After negotiating with European officials, he needed to get final approval from Khamenei. But access to him – for reasons that were never clearly explained – wasn't possible. This delay in communication led to missed opportunities, or more precisely, allowed the Israelis and Americans to take advantage.

There are jokes online. Someone posted a cross-section of Earth and wrote: 'Which layer of the Earth's crust is the Leader hiding in?'

Another has written: 'I thought we'd reached the end of the clerics. Turns out, we've reached the cleric with no end.'

Someone else said, 'They're all the same. Trump was boarding his plane when he said, "China can buy oil from Iran". But the next day, he made the sanctions even harsher. All they care about is making headlines.'

On my way home, I was able to scroll through Instagram and Facebook. One post said that when a Revolutionary Guard base in Karaj was hit, the casualties were so high that people declared that 'the soldiers were flying through the air – you could see them.'

Iran International TV reported that Israel had carried out 1,500 airstrikes into Iranian airspace and hit 1,480 targets, as opposed to 550 ballistic missiles and nearly 1,000 fired by Iran at Israel, 90 per cent of which were inter-cepted, according to figures available on the internet. Meanwhile, on Iranian state television the news subtitles read: 'We no longer permit foreign powers to interfere or negotiate regard-ing uranium enrichment within our territory.' This was followed by a quote from the vice president: 'We learned important lessons from these twelve days.'

Well, for us, the ordinary people, one lesson was that the Basij stopped cars in the middle of highways for random searches – just in case they were carrying helicopters. Another was that oil, rice and other essentials vanished from store shelves. This is what many of us lived through, while officials talked about the 'great achievements' of the war.

At Ferdowsi Square, flags were going up for the start of Muharram, Islamic New Year, with posters announcing religious speakers. I went down into the metro. The escalators weren't working. People were quiet. The only sound was the horn from the train echoing through the tunnel.

These days, the condition of being Persian defies simple categories. It's full of deep contra-dictions about one's country: caught between pride in a rich, cultural past and shame over the current political reality; torn between the push and pull – to stay or to leave. These feelings are shaped by a kind of internal exile – even while you're in your own home. You grieve for stran-gers killed in a war not of your choosing, and worry for older family members and friends who still believe in a dream that has turned into a vicious nightmare.

In such circumstances, the silence around you is freighted: every word and feeling hangs suspended in a turmoil of paradoxes.

Meanwhile, as state media celebrated a victory, the streets looked like someone just out of surgery – wounded in a way that felt neither triumphant nor hopeful, but weak and dazed. Tehran was like a body still under anaesthesia. In the shadows, people walked with tired eyes. Everyone was just searching for something to calm them down. A little peace. A little silence.

When I came out of the metro, a warm wind was blowing. A thin layer of smoke hung in the air, like a sheer curtain draped over the face of the city.

On the way home, I called a friend who had fled to the north. 'I had a Bank Sepah account,' they said. 'During all that chaos, they hacked and froze all the accounts. No withdrawals, no payments, nothing. For a whole week, we just stared at a locked bank card and an empty fridge.'

They went on: 'Same thing happened with

Bank Melli. Everyone was stuck – no money, no updates, no idea what was going on.'

Someone else said, 'We left for Isfahan the moment they told people to evacuate Tehran. But four days later, my sister called. Her son had a panic attack and was taken to the hospital. We got back on the road. But by the time we arrived he was gone. He was thirty-five. Just got married. There was nothing left of him but fear. It was like fear itself had killed him.' I had known this man since he was a boy.

My brother's daughter, just five years old, jumps at the sound of a glass dropping. She clings to the wall, trembling. No one ever told her what war means. But she's learned to recognise the sounds. When someone says, 'It was a cyber-attack,' she believes a monster is coming.

Seemingly, the war has fallen from the sky right into the minds of our children. And me? Every night, when I see a bright dot in the sky, I still wonder: 'Is that a drone … or just a star?'

7

LOOKING FOR A JOB, LIVING AND DYING

May 2025

I tilted my head, waiting for the medication prescribed by my doctor to trickle down into my ear. But before it did, my landlady started shouting, 'Raha! *Venez voir ça! L'Iran a attaqué Israël!'*

Two weeks had passed since I'd bought my ticket back to Iran. Since then, the news had been flooded with images of missiles and drones launched by Iran in retaliation for an Israeli attack. However, my decision had been made. Fourteen years in broom-closet-sized rooms, putting up with eccentric landlords, and unending, repetitive job interviews leading nowhere had exhausted me.

Also, I was worried about my father; his Alzheimer's had worsened. From our frequent phone calls, I could tell that even speaking to me would soon become difficult for him. I remembered one day, years ago, when his illness had already started taking its toll. I found him wandering around the house, searching for something. 'What are you looking for?' I asked.

'Myself,' he replied.

Maybe that was another reason I was going back to my country – to find myself.

Flights from Paris to Iran usually arrived around midnight, but due to the escalating tensions between Iran and Israel, there were frequent delays and changes in schedule. We made our final descent around midday. Outside the window, the bright sunlight illuminated the dry, cracked land that surrounded the towns and cities like the wrinkles on an old man's face. Despite the arid dustiness, the sight of home still moved me; I felt a mixture of love, fear and hope.

My brother picked me up from the airport. It was late September. Even from a distance, Tehran looked calm and familiar. People walked through the streets, heads down. My hand outside of the open car window caressed the warm breeze. It smelled like home.

My mother had rented out the house where I had spent my childhood and moved to a new neighbourhood. When she opened the door, she appeared to have shrunk, her face more worn since I'd seen her a year ago when I'd visited for two weeks.

My father was sitting in his usual chair. He showed no reaction to my arrival.

'Salam,' I greeted him.

He lifted his head momentarily and responded good-naturedly, as was his usual habit. Then, just as quickly, he lowered his head again.

My first week back was mostly spent visiting my brothers and sisters, and, of course, fixing my teeth.

Our family dentist isn't regarded as the best in his field, but his warmth and personality have made him incredibly popular. His clinic is always packed. He works double shifts, assisted by young, cheerful women with whom he shares an easy camaraderie. One said, 'I'm getting a lip piercing today.' The doctor glanced at her, and then looked down at me in the dentist's chair. With a grin he asked, 'Weren't you scared to come back to Iran when they're sending water heaters disguised as missiles towards Israel?'

With his implements in my mouth, I could only nod – a gesture that could mean both yes and no. He charged me 5 million tomans ($50) for a crown.

Afterwards my mother told me, 'Considering how quickly he gave you an appointment, that's a good price.'

I had always wanted to teach at a university, but my bachelor's degree wasn't enough for Iran's University of Art. So, six years ago, I applied for a master's programme at the Paris University of the Arts and got accepted. Before I had finished my studies there, however, COVID hit, and then two years slipped by. By the time five years had passed, I figured it was time to try to realise my dream of teaching art in Iran.

This time, I had a master's degree – with *distinction*. I just needed to talk to the head of the art department at the university. A meeting was arranged in Tehran at my friend's café, where I met two departmental heads, both of whom were enthusiastic about my degree and the possibility of me teaching. We then moved onto the topic of payment. I was stunned. University lecturers earn 35,000 tomans (35 cents) an hour – not even enough to cover transport costs. Essentially, I'd be working for free. And the strangest part? Many people were already doing just that.

I turned to one of the professors: 'If you ask a handyman to change a light bulb in your house, he'll charge you 500,000 ($5) for an hour's work. But a university professor is 35,000?'

He shrugged, 'That's the standard rate for freelance lecturers in all the universities across the country.'

By then, night had fallen, and the three of us could see glowing objects moving across the sky.

A loud voice in the café quipped, 'Looks like Iran is launching more missiles towards Israel.'

But no one seemed too concerned. A quick glance, a passing comment, and then everyone went back to drinking their tea.

The next morning, I walked through my old neighbourhood. It was alive, full of middle-class families; this had been one of the most politically active areas during protests against the government in 2009. I decided to reach out to old friends, some of whom had distanced themselves over the years, assuming I was living comfortably in France, far removed from their struggles. But most were happy to meet up again.

Two of them ran an advertising agency, and one told me that he made $1,500 to $2,000 per month – a great income for Iran. He had also invested in property and was making money from rentals. He was obviously living comfortably and could even afford to travel abroad.

On the opposite end of the spectrum was Zeina, a painter I've known for thirty years. She had never managed to afford even a small apartment, and had blamed her husband for their economic situation. Six years ago, when I was back in the country, I'd sensed that her feelings for him had faded, but at that point she hadn't had the courage to leave him. Now, when we met, she proudly showed me the stamp in her ID: 'Two weeks ago, I got divorced.'

To secure it, she had waived her *mehrieh*, a cash payment to the wife in religious marriages, and this made it easier for her husband to agree to a legal separation. Due to the soaring cost of rent, however, the two of them were still living under the same roof. She was unable to answer the question of how to make a living while working in the arts.

Two universities invited me to speak about my experiences abroad. The atmosphere on campus was nothing like it was when I was a student. Twenty years ago, young men and women had separate staircases. Now I saw women attending classes without their mandatory hijabs, and freely socialising with their male classmates.

After my lecture I received an invitation from a department head to teach art history there. But the pay was the same – 35,000 tomans an hour.

According to him, permanent faculty members on the university's payroll earned between 30 and 40 million tomans – around $300 to $400 per month. Considering Iran's high living costs, even this wasn't an adequate wage. And when I asked him if there was any possibility of getting a permanent position at the university, he sighed: 'I've been teaching here for twenty years, and I'm still on a temporary contract.'

What struck me about this man was that despite his religious background he was openly against the government. 'If a student wants to create art on campus,' he told me, 'we have to submit an official request.' He also said that during the Woman, Life, Freedom protests, many of his students had been beaten up by the security forces.

Before I left the country, I had had only a couple of chances at securing stable employment, and on both occasions I'd failed the religious screening because I had answered questions honestly. Now that I was looking again, I met up with an old flame, Laila, who had recently begun looking for a new job too and was happy to share her experiences.

When we first knew each other, Laila used to call my college dorm weekly, which led me to be kicked out of student housing. Like me, she had always failed government screening when applying for permanent employment. But this time, she said, the process felt different. 'Back then, I was young and naïve – I didn't understand the system. Even though I wore a long manteau coat, a headscarf and no make-up, they treated me horribly. But this time, I realised that the people handling the employment screenings are stuck in their own little world. They give you forms full of religious and ideological questions, and you have to answer them in a way that doesn't raise suspicions.'

She continued, 'My sister coached me on what to say. I lied about almost everything – I wrote that I don't have an Instagram account, I don't own a passport, and so on.' For her interview, she wore a full *maghna*, a formal scarf that fully covers the head and neck, mostly worn by women who work in government institutions. At the end, the woman in charge of recruitment smiled warmly as she took Laila's papers and said, 'I'm so happy to have met you.'

Walking with Laila through Tehran, it was impossible not to notice that most young women no longer bothered with headscarves. Just a few years ago they were prohibited from cycling, and now some of them speed through the city streets, the wind in their hair.

Autumn is the season of art in the city, and new exhibitions were opening one after another. I had gone with a friend to northern Tehran to see one. In the taxi on the way there I could see how the city had changed. Despite the sanctions and inflation, new shopping malls towered over the streets – gleaming glass facades, symbols of wealth and modernity. New highways had been built yet the traffic was as suffocating as ever. A trip that should have taken thirty minutes dragged on for hours, with the app on our phones showing a sea of red lines as the veins of the metropolis throbbed with congestion.

As we waited in the traffic, my friend and I talked about American foreign policy. Suddenly, the taxi driver interrupted. 'Don't worry, sir!' he said, 'Things can't possibly get worse than this. Maybe Trump is actually the Mahdi himself, here to save the world from misery!'

Making jokes about religious figures in Iran can be a risky business. That evening, I met up with another old friend, and he told me about his seventeen-year-old son, who had been arrested during the Woman, Life, Freedom protests. The security forces had hacked into his son's phone and sent messages to the boy's friends to lure them into a trap. Everyone was arrested. After days of frantic searching, my friend finally discovered where his son was being held.

During the trial, the judge said that the case

against the boy was serious, not only because he had been protesting, but because his phone was filled with anti-government slogans mocking Islam and Iran's Supreme Leader. For three weeks, my friend visited the courts daily, desperately searching for a way to save his son from a lengthy prison sentence.

Eventually, with the right connections and plenty of pleading, he found an officer willing to erase the data from his son's phone and return it to him. This is what saved him.

In the negotiations with the boy's father, the officer also revealed something chilling. 'During the protests,' he told my friend, 'our forces walk among the crowds wearing special wristwatches with hidden cameras, recording everything. That's how we identify and arrest people later.'

The next day in Enghelab Square, the streets were eerily empty, most of the shops closed. I stopped by a newspaper stand and asked the vendor why everything was shut. 'Because of air pollution!' he replied.

The pollution was intense – I could feel a burning sensation in my lungs. Every two weeks Tehran shut down because of the hazardous air quality. Even restrictions like the traffic control plan had failed to make a difference. Power outages too occurred nearly every other day, and schools, banks and government offices were closed. The official reasons were either energy shortages or government-imposed shutdowns to save electricity. This hadn't been the case six years ago.

That night my brother called to tell me that my father had fallen ill during the night and been taken to hospital. I rushed there as quickly as I could, and found my mother, distressed, standing by his bed. She said the doctor had diagnosed a severe bloodstream infection and that my father needed to be transferred to the ICU. But no beds were available. If we moved him to another hospital, the bed he currently occupied would be lost.

I told my family I would stay with him that night and that they should go home and return in shifts the next day. When I asked a nurse if there was any possibility of transferring my father to the ICU, she pointed to another patient in the ward and said, 'That man has been waiting for days, and there's still no free bed. If we had one, he would have gone first.'

By afternoon the next day my siblings had arrived. So I went home to rest, returning later that evening, when my mother and brother changed my father's diaper while I emptied his urine bag in the bathroom.

A half hour later I was alone by his bedside. I stared at his face and hands. His muscles had wasted away, leaving only skin and bones. He was on oxygen, his vitals monitored on a screen.

Suddenly, shouting erupted from the main hall. The patient who had been scheduled for an ICU bed before my father had been transferred there but was now being returned to the ward. His furious son was yelling, 'This man is a war veteran! He was injured in a chemical attack! And this is how you treat him?' He and his brother had travelled from a nearby town and had been waiting for four days. They were taking turns sleeping in their car.

The hospital staff wheeled the man's bed next to my father's. Waves of exhaustion swept over me. When I'd gone home earlier in the day I'd been unable to sleep. Around 1 a.m., my father suddenly began to tremble violently. His teeth clenched; his eyes rolled back. I called to him but he didn't respond.

The nurses' station in the ward was empty so I ran into the main hall. No one was there. I shouted, and finally a nurse emerged from a room. Desperate, I told her that my father was having a seizure. We ran back together and, when she saw him, she immediately went for help, returning with other nurses. They rolled my father onto his side and injected him with medication. Slowly, his convulsions eased, his breathing heavy and ragged.

One nurse said, 'His lungs are full of fluid.' They inserted a suction tube into his mouth, and I could hear the sound of liquid being drawn out. Finally, a doctor arrived and examined him.

When I asked the nurse what had caused my father's seizure, she said it might have been a reaction to the antibiotics. She replaced the oxygen tubes in his nose with a plastic mask. Then the lights were turned off and the nurses left. The relatives of other patients, who had been disturbed by all the commotion, dozed off once again in their chairs.

I remained awake and watchful, fearful that it might happen again. My father kept pulling his blanket off, and I repeatedly covered him up. He would also remove his oxygen mask, which I would then readjust. We went back and forth like this for the next two hours until he suddenly had another powerful seizure.

I ran back to the main hall, coming back with a nurse who added a sedative to my father's IV. He finally fell into a deep sleep.

At 6 a.m., the cleaning staff arrived to mop the floors. A nurse walked through the ward and straightened the patients' blankets. 'The morning shift will be here soon,' she said to no one in particular, 'and everything has to look neat and clean.'

I was extremely tired when my mother and brother arrived mid-morning. In passing, my brother said, 'On my way here I ran into a doctor I know. I think he's in charge of the ICU.'

It was an opportunity we dared not miss. 'Please, if you can, ask him to transfer Dad to the ICU. He's been paying insurance for years and has every type. If we don't use it now, when will we?'

I arrived back at the hospital that evening. Then, thankfully, my brother called to say that he'd spoken to the doctor and that Dad was to be transferred to the ICU. After my mother and one of my brothers arrived the next morning, two nurses started moving my father's bed towards the elevator. When we tried to go with him, they stopped us: 'Only one person can accompany us, and visiting days are limited to two days a week, with only two people allowed in at a time.'

I had already spent the night with Dad so I told my mother and brother to go ahead while I waited outside. When they returned from the ICU, they told me, 'He's breathing 50 per cent with a machine, and his blood pressure is very low.'

On the days when we couldn't visit we called in to check on him. The next time we were allowed back was on Tuesday, and my mother, one of my brothers and I went to the hospital. Again, I let the others go into the ICU, but this time I asked the security guard if I could see my father for just a few seconds. He said it was impossible.

I had to wait until Sunday. On Friday, when we called the hospital, the nurse reported that 'your father is almost better, he opened his eyes and should be discharged soon.' Our happiness, however, was tinged with concern: how were we going to take care of him at home? My brother called the doctor who was familiar with my father's case, and he reassured him that it wasn't yet time for Dad to be discharged; we shouldn't worry.

Sunday came, and to enter the ICU I changed into protective clothing. The unit was full of beds. When I saw my father I called out to him, but he was unable to turn his head. So I moved to the other side of the bed. 'How are you?', I asked.

His eyes filled with tears and panic. It was so hard to see him in such pain. I felt as though he were hanging over a cliff, waiting for the moment he would let go and fall into the abyss.

They called us the next Sunday morning and told us to bring the necessary papers. It was a sign: this visit was to be our final goodbye. Dad was now completely dependent on a machine to breathe, and his heart rate had dropped significantly.

Around 8 p.m. that evening, we received the call that he had passed away. We had to come the next morning and pick up his body. The hospital where I had been born was the very place my father had died.

That night, we decided to bury him next to his father, in a plot our family has had permission to use for the past thirty years. The cost of buying a new one was exorbitant.

During the burial ceremony, I realised that many people buy a grave in a cemetery before they die. Graves have become an investment because land, for the living and the dead in Iran, has become increasingly expensive. A friend told me that he needed an eye for his mother, and was told that a cemetery worker, who washes bodies before burial, sold the eyes of the recently deceased. After several visits, he managed to obtain one from a corpse to bring home.